This study project aims to educate the public about administrative professionals and their invaluable roles in the workplace.

CAREER CHOICES FOR ADMINISTRATIVE PROFESSIONALS

PETER OVIE AKUS

PATHWAYS COLLEGE 205 HORTON STREET, LONDON, ON N6B 1K7

TABLE OF CONTENTS

....0
ACKNOWLEDGEMENTS..2
DEDICATION 3
INTRODUCTION 4
DUTIES OF AN ADMINISTRATIVE PROFESSIONAL 5
HOW TO BECOME AN ADMINISTRATIVE PROFESSIONAL 6
CLASSES OF ADMINISTRATIVE PROFESSIONALS 7
TYPES OF ADMINISTRATIVE PROFESSIONALS...8
SECRETARY...9
DUTIES OF A SECRETARY..10
SKILLS OF A SECRETARY 11
INCOME OF A SECRETARY..12
CLERK 13
DUTIES OF A CLERK..14
SKILLS OF A CLERK 15
INCOME OF A CLERK..16
RECEPTIONIST 17
DUTIES OF A RECEPTIONIST 18
SKILLS OF A RECEPTIONIST...19
INCOME OF A RECEPTIONIST 20
DATE ENTRY ASSISTANT 21
DUTIES OF A DATA ENTRY ASSISTANT...22
SKILLS OF A DATA ENTRY ASSISTANT 23
INCOME OF A DATA ENTRY ASSISTANT...24
CUSTOMER SERVICE REPRESENTATIVE 25
DUTIES OF A CUSTOMER SERVICE REPRESENTATIVE 26
SKILLS OF A CUSTOMER SERVICE REPRESENTATIVE..27
INCOME OF A CUSTOMER SERVICE REPRESENTATIVE 28
CONCLUSION...29
BIBLIOGRAPHY 30

ACKNOWLEDGEMENTS

I acknowledge the facilitator of the ACT Program at Pathways College, London, Ontario, Canada, Marci Allen-Easton, as the muse behind this book. I thank her for everything she has taught me, and most importantly for encouraging my writing. I am eternally indebted to her because her inspiration and encouragement has put fire back in my fingers, especially at a time when I was thinking of turning my back on this divine deposit and pursuing other endeavors.

I thank Laurie Rintoul, Corrina MacDonald, Ariana Pilolli, and the entire staff and management at PATHWAYS for the scholarship that was given to me alongside all the other freebies like laptop, designer clothes, bus tickets, among other things which enabled me to study smoothly and graduate with distinction.

I thank supportive classmates like Nyemal Kueth, Akol Angou, Sarah Kosgei, Laura Morke, Mackenzie Lavalliere, Kelly Bourne, Cassandra Renaud and everyone whose name I can't remember. You ladies are the best.

DEDICATION

I dedicate this book to my baby, Esther Estelle Akus, for believing in me, and supporting me at a time when everyone ran away.

INTRODUCTION

Some of you might probably be seeing the word "administrative professionals" for the first time in your life. Others might have heard of it but have never really given much thought to what it really means due to inherent assumptions which might be right or wrong. However, it is a truism that assumptions are the lowest form of knowledge. The critical question is, who is an administrative professional?

According to the latest Canadian census (Career Professionals of Canada, 2020), there are more than 1.8 million administrative professionals working in Canada. It is my fervent belief that at the end of this paper, the reader would be fully educated about administrative professionals and the invaluable roles that they play in the workplace.

Brenna Goyette, a career expert, defines an administrative professional as someone responsible for providing support to an organization. They handle a variety of tasks, including scheduling appointments, maintaining records, and handling correspondence. Administrative professionals are often the first point of contact for customers and clients, so they must be able to communicate effectively (Goyette, 2022).

In lay terms, we can refer to administrative professionals as support workers in an organization. They are ubiquitous and there are very few people upon the face of the earth who have not benefited in one way or form from the services that they render. Examples of administrative professionals include but are not limited to; Executive Assistants, Secretaries, Clerks, Receptionists, Office Managers, and Customer Service Representatives.

An administrative professional is someone who helps an organization accomplish its goals efficiently. They exist in a variety of capacities, working for companies and in roles where their specific duties depend on the type of business or institution employing them. In most settings, administrative professionals create short-term and long-term strategies to ensure successful operations, establish objectives, and organize initiatives. They oversee processes and facilitate business functions to keep everything running smoothly and efficiently.

A better way to understand everything I have tried to describe in this introduction, is to simply have it at the back of your mind, that an administrative professional is a professional that supports administration in an organization.

DUTIES OF AN ADMINISTRATIVE PROFESSIONAL

The duties of an administrative professional may slightly differ from one another due to the various job types but they are all geared towards the same objective which is providing support services in an organization. Some of the common ones include:

- Attending to visitors: There are very few organizations on earth today that do not have a front desk that attends to visitors among other functions. Even in large apartment buildings, you will still find a front desk that attends to visitors and directs residents on what to do whenever they need help. The people who man the front desks are called receptionists and they are skilled in interpersonal communication.

- Scheduling appointments: This is the function of people we call executive assistants or personal assistants. They help managers and other key administrators in an organization manage their schedule which in turn translates into smooth running of the organization.

- Maintaining records: They are the bookkeepers. They are also called clerks or secretaries depending on the appellation favored by an organization. Their primary duty is to keep records both manually and online so that they can be easily reproduced whenever they are needed.

- Making and receiving phone calls: This function is mostly performed by the people who man the front desk – the receptionists. It is also performed by other administrative professionals in the workplace depending on need and function.

- Handling correspondence: It is the duty of an administrative professional to handle correspondence i.e., letters, mails, memos, etc. sent to and from an organization, either online or offline. This can be done by secretaries, clerks, receptionists, etcetera.

HOW TO BECOME AN ADMINISTRATIVE PROFESSIONAL

There are three major steps towards becoming an administrative professional.

The first step is computer literacy. It is a sine qua non for anyone who desires to become an administrative professional. This is because the modern-day workplace is run digitally therefore ignorance of basic computer skills is a great disadvantage. If you desire to become an administrative professional but know nothing about computers, are advanced in age, aside other impediments, you can easily enroll in a short course at any educational institute (like PATHWAYS) and you will be taught the basics. Beyond becoming an administrative professional, computer literacy is a must for everyone in this 21st century as almost everything pertaining to life and living revolves around computers. It is pertinent for me to state that computer literacy is not rocket science and can easily be learnt by anyone irrespective of your aptitude or cognitive ability.

The second step is the possession of soft skills like communication, time management, attention to detail, organizational skills, emotional intelligence, multi-tasking, etc. Some people have these skills naturally e.g., women but for others they have to be learnt. These skills which look unimportant on the surface, are what will ensure success in your career as an administrative professional. You might claim ignorance of these skills but if you enroll in any course for training administrative professionals (like ACT program at PATHWAYS), you will be taught these skills and how to deploy them in the workplace.

The third and final step is formal education. By formal education, I mean the ability to read and write proficiently. This is absolutely necessary as much of your duties as an administrative professional revolves around reading and writing. Even in administrative professionals that require some technical knowledge, for example, medical secretary, you still need to be well versed in reading and writing in the language of instruction in your country. In bilingual countries like Canada, you might choose one depending on the province in which you are domiciled but you have a very clear advantage if you are proficient in both. A High School Diploma is a basic requirement as proof of literacy.

CLASSES OF ADMINISTRATIVE PROFESSIONALS

There are three classes of administrative professionals. Every administrative professional fall into one of these three classes. It is impossible to cite every administrative job that exist in the workplace as responsibilities, functions, duties, and organizational structures differs from one organization to another. The three classes of administrative professionals are:

1. Entry-level administrative professional: They perform a wide variety of functions which ensure the smooth operation of the office and also provide support to other members of an organization. For the records, much of the focus of this discourse will be on entry-level administrative jobs. Examples of this type of administrators are Office Assistant, Data Entry Clerk, Receptionist, Office Administrator, and Events Administrator.

2. Mid-level administrative professional: This is a notch higher than the entry-level administrative professional. They perform a smaller number of more specialized tasks in the office using the experience they have gained as entry-level administrators. Mid-level administrative professionals are responsible for creating and maintaining organizational policies which improves operations in a company. Examples of this type of administrators are Operations Manager, Executive Assistant, Facilities Manager, Office Manager, Administrative Technician, Service Administrator, Administrative Services Manager, Business Administrator, Staff Assistant, Front Desk Supervisor, and Senior Administrative Analyst.

3. Upper-level administrative professional: This is the highest level of administrative professionals. They mainly perform deeper and more specialized work. Their responsibilities are more focused and specific. Examples of this type of administrators are Chief Administrative Officer, Senior Executive Assistant, Community Liaison, Senior Personal Assistant, Chief People Officer, and Chief Operating Officer.

It is pertinent to state that it is possible for someone to move from the entry-level administrative professional to the highest class of upper-level administrative professional. What is required is additional trainings and efficiency at the workplace. Sometimes, you might need to join professional associations like the Association of Administrative Professionals (AAP) in Canada to get more certifications.

TYPES OF ADMINISTRATIVE PROFESSIONALS

In this section, we'll begin to take an in-depth look at some administrative professionals, as well as their duties, skills, and rewards. The following administrators will be my focus:

- Secretary
- Clerk
- Receptionist
- Data Entry Assistant
- Customer Service Representative

SECRETARY	CLERK	RECEPTIONIST
DATA ENTRY ASSISTANT	CUSTOMER SERVICE REPRESENTATIVE	

SECRETARY

A secretary is an administrative professional that supports management including executives, using a variety of project management, program evaluation, communication, and organizational skills within the area of administration (Wikipedia contributors, 2024). It is necessary to state that secretary as an administrative assistant is different from the role of Executive Secretary, Cabinet Secretary, Company Secretary or any other title that has secretary attached to them. Though they have the appellation of secretary appended to them, the roles that they play in an organization differ vastly from those played by the secretary who is an administrative assistant.

Judging by the etymology of the word secretary, it is obvious that in ancient times, a secretary is someone that can be described as a confidante or a keeper of secrets. Even now that we are in the technological age, a secretary must be someone who can keep confidences because they are generally in charge of communications in an organization. They are the ones who draft memos, letters, contracts, etcetera. If there are leaks of information in any organization, the secretaries are most times likely responsible for it.

Secretaries must possess certain qualities like being well-organized, hardworking, resourceful, persistent, detail-oriented, and a strong drive to make things work. They are responsible for preparing documents, spreadsheets, organize files, and schedule appointments. They handle administration activities in places like school, healthcare facilities, government offices, and private companies.

Secretaries are often referred to as administrative assistants. Most people use the word interchangeably and to some when you mention the word administrative assistant, what comes to their mind is the image of a secretary.

DUTIES OF A SECRETARY

This list is by no means exhaustive. The roles played by a secretary is greatly dependent on the structure of the organization. These are just some of the basic roles that are often ascribed to secretaries in most organizations.

- ❖ Answering and directing phone calls and organizing and distributing messages
- ❖ Scheduling and arranging meetings, events, accommodation, and other appointments for management and staff
- ❖ Preparing, copying, faxing, and filing documents and correspondence
- ❖ Greeting and assisting business clients and guests
- ❖ Documenting and managing financial information and office supplies

DUTIES OF A SECRETARY

SKILLS OF A SECRETARY

The following skills are a necessity for a good secretary:

- Communication: You need to be proficient in verbal and written communication. This is extremely necessary because you will be in charge of the flow of information in an organization. Clear communication allows you to relay important information between guests, customers, colleagues, and executives.

- Computer Skills: Your computer skills must be topnotch. You must be proficient in the use of web apps like Microsoft Word, Microsoft Outlook, Microsoft Excel and Microsoft Power point. You must also be well versed in the use of email. Ability to learn new things is essential as the rate of knowledge is increasing greatly and new technologies are invented every year. For example, ten years ago, nobody was talking about Artificial Intelligence. Today, it is on the lips of everybody.

- Typing and Notetaking: Typing is something that cannot be avoided in the office environment. You must be skilled in typing as there will be plenty of documents to be typed daily or weekly as the case may be. Closely related to this is notetaking. It is a skill that is important as secretaries often sit in on meetings with their bosses and keep a record of what was said and by whom.

- Organization and time management: You must be able to manage schedules, coordinate meetings and maintain filing systems. This skill is fundamental because it ensures the smooth running of an organization by avoiding disorganization as everything is done by the books. Secretaries are in charge of bookkeeping and filing of records. Therefore, paying attention to details is also important to avoid any disruption in the system.

- Customer Service: This might appear far-fetched but as a secretary you must know how to relate with difficult people and manage conflict. You will be relating with customers, guests, colleagues, and your bosses, and as it is with all human interactions, you will inevitably encounter conflict and difficult people. Your interpersonal skills must be avant-garde.

INCOME OF A SECRETARY

The average annual income of a secretary in Canada is $44,850. This translates into $23 per hour. Entry-level positions start at $37,063. However, secretaries with years of experience can earn as high as $54,272 per year. Below is a chart showing the income of secretaries in the various provinces in Canada.

(talent.com, 2024)

CLERK

Collins Dictionary defines a clerk as a person who works in an office, bank, or law court and whose job is to look after the records or accounts (Collins Dictionary, n.d.). I chose this definition because a lot of people actually conflate clerks with secretaries. This could also be due to the fact that clerks also carry out secretarial duties in most organizations. But they are not one and the same.

Clerks are primarily recordkeepers. They not only keep records but also accounts. This does not mean that they are accountants. It is the job of the accountant to prepare the account but the duty of the clerk to store the record of the accounts as drawn by the accountant. In other words, they keep financial records. They record and file all kinds of information which makes it easy for them to reproduce whenever it is needed or required. Any organization without a clerk would find it difficult to exist or run smoothly without hinderance or let. Below is an example of records from Pathways Career College's Administrative and Clerical Training Program (Summer Class of 2024).

NAME OF STUDENT	COURSE OF STUDY
PETER OVIE AKUS	ACT PROGRAM
NYEMAL KUETH	ACT PROGRAM
AKOL ANGOU	ACT PROGRAM
KELLY BOURNE	ACT PROGRAM
ANDREA PINCHETE	ACT PROGRAM
CASSANDRA RENAUD	ACT PROGRAM
LAURA MORKE	ACT PROGRAM

DUTIES OF A CLERK

- ✓ Maintain files and records so they remain updated and easily accessible.
- ✓ Sort and distribute incoming mail and prepare outgoing mail (envelopes, packages, etc.)
- ✓ Answer the phone to take messages or redirect calls to appropriate colleagues.
- ✓ Utilize office appliances such as photocopier, printers etc. and computers for word processing, spreadsheet creation etc.
- ✓ Undertake basic bookkeeping tasks and issue invoices, checks etc.
- ✓ Take minutes of meetings and dictations.
- ✓ Assist in office management and organization procedures.
- ✓ Monitor stocks of office supplies (paper clips, stationery etc.) and report when there are shortages.
- ✓ Assist in making travel arrangements and booking venues for conferences and events.
- ✓ Perform other office duties as assigned **(Bika, n.d.)**

SKILLS OF A CLERK

Clerks perform mostly secretarial duties and I do not want to sound like a broken record by repeating the same skills that I have written about under the skills required by secretaries. So, I will focus on the core skills required by clerks based on their primary role as recordkeepers.

- Proficiency in Mathematics: This skill is non-negotiable for anyone who aspires to be a clerk. You must be comfortable with figures or else you will mess up a lot of things. This doesn't mean that you should be a math genius before becoming a clerk. It only means that basic calculations shouldn't give you headaches.

- Meticulous and Thorough: This borders on temperament even though it is a skill that can be imbibed. You shouldn't be tardy or haphazard. You must know how to pay attention to details and how to thoroughly scrutinize. And to ask the right questions which can help you easily get the data that you require. If you file records wrongly, a lot of damage would be done which would take a lot of effort to repair.

- Proficiency with Computers: You need to be good at storing records on computers. The records that are stored must be done in such a way that it is easily retrievable.

- Confidential: A good clerk isn't flippant. As the recordkeeper of an organization, you are often privy to information which many others are not including some of your bosses. Mum should be your watchword as leaks could lead to distrust, gossips, envy, bitterness, and even the downfall of an organization under certain circumstances.

- Knowledgeable: This doesn't presuppose that you must be a polymath to become a clerk. It means that you must be knowledgeable and willing to learn, if need be, by asking questions. Assumptions are a huge risk which could be costly in the long run. For example, imagine filing a record on the computer as "London, United Kingdom" instead of "London, Ontario" because you are unaware of another London existing in any other country of the world and are too proud to ask or seek clarification. Therefore, all correspondence with that company would be sent to the wrong address.

INCOME OF A CLERK

The average annual salary for a clerk in Canada is $36,710. This translates into $18.83 per hour. Entry-level positions start at $30,225 annually. Workers with years of experience can make as much as $49,674 annually. Below is a chart showing the annual wages of a clerk in various Canadian provinces.

Clerk: salaries per region

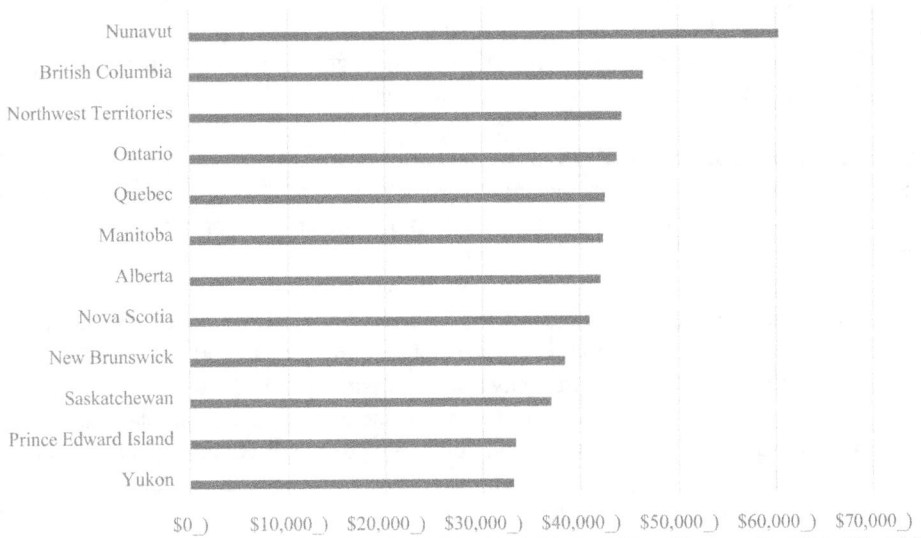

(talent.com, 2024)

RECEPTIONIST

A receptionist is a front-line administrative professional responsible for managing the front desk of an organization. Their primary role involves greeting visitors, answering phone calls, and directing inquiries to the appropriate individuals or departments (Taylor, What is a Receptionist? Introduction, Types, & Skills, 2024).

First impressions matter a lot and the people responsible for generating first impressions on behalf of an organization are the receptionists. They man the front desk and the way that they treat visitors and clients is of utmost importance. Hence, their interpersonal and communication skills must be above average. They should always wear a cheerful and optimistic look and use kind words or else they run the risk of generating bad impressions about an organization in the mind of a potential client or visitor.

Receptionists also handle administrative and clerical duties in an organization. They perform roles like handling correspondence, making and receiving phone calls, and answering to general enquiries from staff and visitors. They are often a liaison between clients, employees, and management.

One great and important role played by receptionists which is often glossed over is security. Though they do not bear arms, they monitor the flow of human traffic in and out of the organization through the aid of computers. They also use their emotional intelligence to assess visitors and determine whether or not to allow them into the building. For example, if someone with mental health issues storms an organization demanding to see the Chief Executive Officer, it is the duty of the receptionist to politely turn them away seeing that they are unwell and might harbour negative intentions towards the CEO.

DUTIES OF A RECEPTIONIST

The following are some of the duties of a receptionist.

- Frontline Desk: Receptionists are the first point of contact in any organization. They man the frontline desk which is a communication hub both for staff and visitors. They greet visitors, clients, and staff and generate positive impressions on behalf of the organization.
- Handling Correspondence and Enquiries: They make and receive phone calls, send and receive emails, and letters, on behalf of the staff and management of an organization. They also handle general or specific enquiries, relay messages, and direct calls to the appropriate individual.
- Appointments: Receptionists are in charge of handling appointments. They schedule appointments and notify staff of changes to appointments as is necessary.
- Assist Visitors: They assist visitors to find their way around a building and to locate the individual whom they seek to do business with. This role is crucial because without receptionists, many would find it difficult to navigate large buildings which most organizations use as offices.
- Administrative role: They play administrative roles like data entry, filing, and maintaining office supplies. They also do book keeping duties.
- Security: Just like I stated earlier, receptionists monitor access to the premises, verify the identity of visitors, and enforce security protocols.

SKILLS OF A RECEPTIONIST

There are three major skills that are required to be a successful receptionist.

1. Typing Skills: This is absolutely essential for all typists as it enables them to carry out their administrative functions efficiently. As a receptionist, you can't avoid sending emails, creating documents, and typing letters and memos. Hence, your typing skills must be excellent because you might have to do lots of these everyday if you work for a large organization.

2. Technical Skills: You must be proficient in the use of various software in computers and other electronic devices like phones and tablets. The modern office environment is highly digitized and the possession of technical skills such as these is necessary especially in the area of scheduling, communications and data entry. I remember working in a large apartment building in America as a receptionist. Whenever we receive mails and other packages intended for occupants of the building, we scan the bar code with an app on an office phone which contains the names and room numbers of all the occupants of the building. The app immediately sends a text message or an email to the recipient informing them that they have a package and should go to the front desk to get it.

3. Customer Service: This skill is a must because it is responsible for generating impressions about the company in the minds of visitors. You must have a cheerful and pleasant attitude as a receptionist. A nice smile, ever willing to help, and give the necessary information as the need arises is the hallmark of an excellent receptionist. Simply put, you cannot afford to be a failure in the area of interpersonal communication.

INCOME OF A RECEPTIONIST

The average annual salary for a receptionist in Canada is $39,000. This translates into $20 per hour. Entry-level positions start at $31,961 per year. Experienced workers can earn up to $46,749 annually. Below, is a chart showing the annual salaries of receptionists in various Canadian provinces.

Receptionist: salaries per region

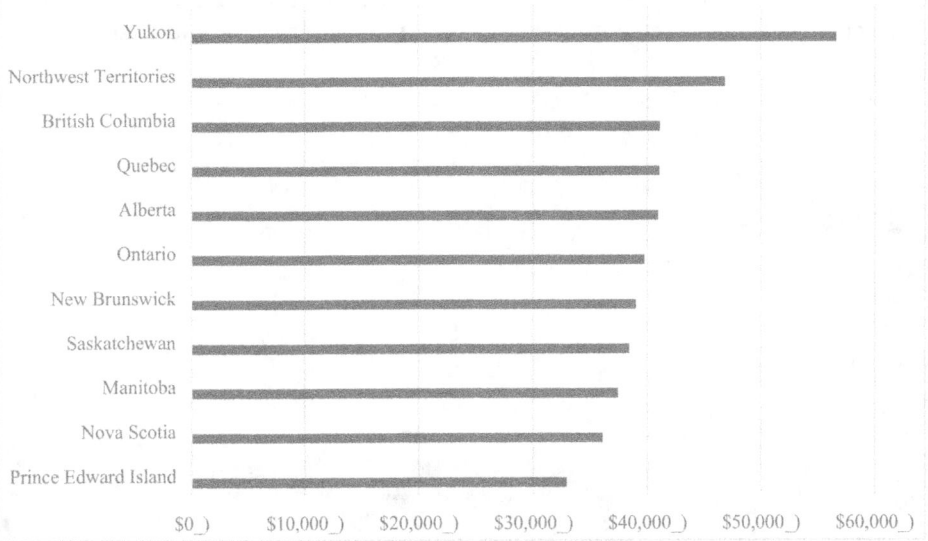

(talent.com, 2024)

DATE ENTRY ASSISTANT

Data Entry Assistants are administrative professionals who input information from handwritten documents, phone calls, or recordings into a computer system in an organized manner. In some organizations, they also perform job duties similar to an administrative assistant like answering phone calls, greeting visitors, and sorting mails.

With the rise of artificial intelligence and other technological innovations, the job of a data entry assistant looks like a dying breed. However, it is still a necessity especially when it comes to the subject of data accuracy and quality control as that can only be done effectively by humans.

DUTIES OF A DATA ENTRY ASSISTANT

- Input data into the computer system
- Update or delete outdated data in the computer system
- Review documents and data reports for accuracy
- Maintain confidentiality
- Assist with other administrative tasks as needed

 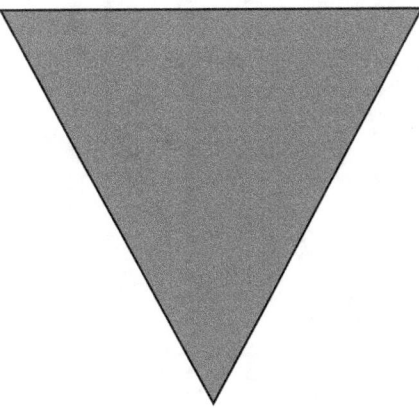

SKILLS OF A DATA ENTRY ASSISTANT

The major skill required for a data entry assistant is typing skills. You must be able to type between 50 to 80 words per minute. The other skills that you need are the same with those of an administrative assistant.

It must be stated that as a data entry assistant you must be able to maintain focus for an extended period of time and pay attention to details as the job requires a high level of accuracy. You can easily improve your typing skills by enrolling for free on this website.

INCOME OF A DATA ENTRY ASSISTANT

The annual average salary of a data entry assistant in Canada is $48,177. This translates into $24.71 per hour. Entry-level positions often start at $36,439 annually. Experienced workers may earn up to $66,250 annually. Below is chart showing the annual salaries of data entry assistants in different Canadian provinces.

Data entry assistant: salaries per year

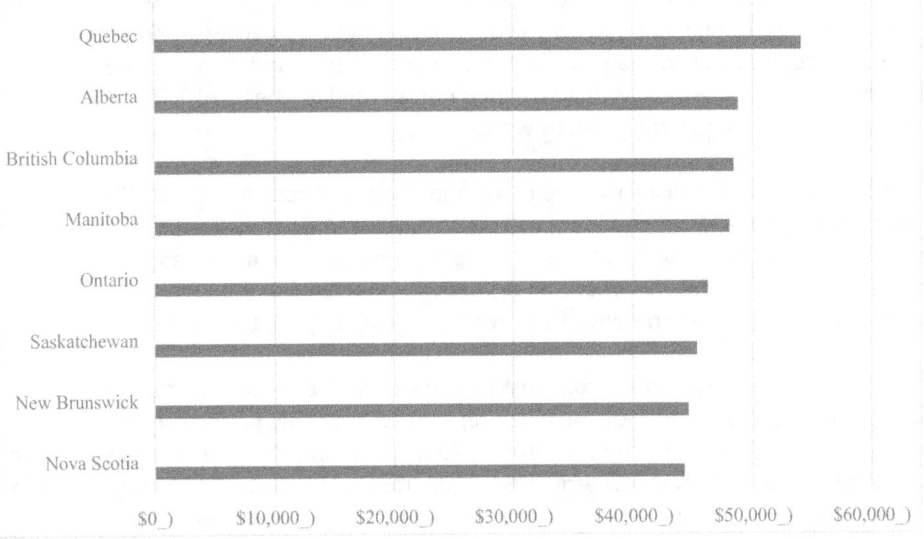

(talent.com, 2024)

CUSTOMER SERVICE REPRESENTATIVE

A Customer Service Representative is the first point of contact for any customer who has a question or an issue with a product or service the company sells (Kourmentza, n.d.). This implies that all companies have or should have a customer service representative.

A customer service representative is a problem-solver. He/she must be a good conversationalist and someone who can speak to people from all works of life. You must be able to handle difficult people because you will encounter many of them daily. In the podcast series, Customer Service Representative (Jenna, n.d.), Jenna the host, details her experiences working as a customer service representative in a grocery store. It contains the good, bad, and the ugly. The message I am trying to pass across is that this job is not for the faint-hearted. It is not for sensitive people who are easily offended by words.

Most times this job involves talking to people over the phone and replying emails. You must be comfortable talking over a long period of time over the phone. A customer service representative occupies a unique position in a company. He has been mandated by the company to resolve the complaints of customers about a product or service offered by the company. He/she needs to use this power wisely and not step beyond their bounds.

As a customer service representative, you must be knowledgeable about the product or service that is sold by your company. And you must be prepared to work long hours resolving complaints daily. Jesse Owens (Farmers Insurance, 2017), a customer service representative for Farmers Insurance, claims he resolves around 80 – 100 transactions daily. This tells you that the job of customer service representative is neither for the weak nor for the faint-hearted.

DUTIES OF A CUSTOMER SERVICE REPRESENTATIVE

These are some of the duties of a customer care representative in an organization.

- Give information about a company's product or service: Every customer service representative must be knowledgeable about the product or service sold by the company. This also includes special offers, promotions, and sales. This will enable you to give quick and satisfactory answers to customers when they call or email to make enquiries.

- Processing orders and transactions: Customer Service Representatives help customers to not only process orders and transactions but also to get refunds, cancellations, and exchanges.

- Trouble shooting: You must be willing to help customer resolve issues that might arise as a result of the use of a product or service. This might involve having a little technical knowledge but if you can't handle it, you can refer the issue to the technical department for resolution.

- Handling complaints: This is inevitable. You will handle complaints and it must be done in a professional manner. It must be done with empathy which is revealed in your choice of words. You don't have to yell back at the customer if they yell at you. Be firm and communicate your words in a clear and calm way. Most importantly, you must make the customer feel that you have done your possible best to resolve the issue.

SKILLS OF A CUSTOMER SERVICE REPRESENTATIVE

Listed below, in no particular order, are 21 skills that must be possessed by every customer service representative.

1. Active listening
2. Adaptability
3. Attention to detail
4. Collaboration
5. Conflict resolution
6. Creativity
7. Critical thinking
8. Decision-making
9. Effective communication
10. Emotional intelligence
11. Empathy
12. Friendliness
13. Negotiation skills
14. Open-mindedness
15. Patience
16. Persuasion
17. Problem-solving
18. Product knowledge
19. Time management
20. Understanding body language
21. Writing skills

(Eads, 2024)

INCOME OF A CUSTOMER SERVICE REPRESENTATIVE

On the average, a customer service representative in Canada earns $39,069 annually. This translates into $20.04 per hour. Entry-level positions start at $32,179, while experienced workers can earn up to $52,570. Below is a chart showing the salaries of customer service representatives in various Canadian provinces.

Customer service representative: salaries per region

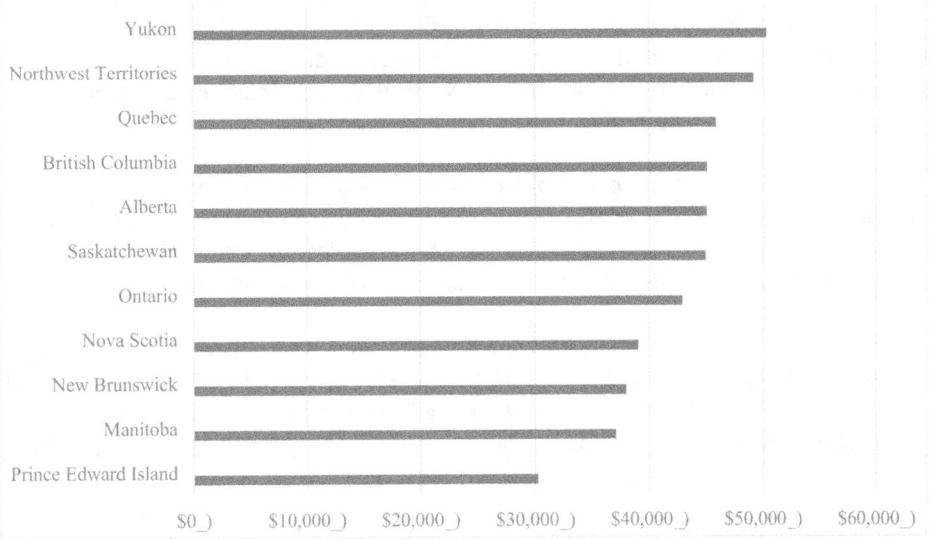

(talent.com, 2024)

CONCLUSION

My preferred administrative professional is the SECRETARY. These are my reasons.

Firstly, it is the apex administrative professional job, not because it is sometimes called administrative assistant to confer some sort of dignity on it, but because a secretary can perform optimally in all types of administrative jobs including those which I have cited and those I haven't. A secretary by virtue of his/her training can play the role of a clerk, receptionist, data entry assistant, and customer service representative. As a matter of fact, most secretaries play some of these roles in most organizations in addition to their assigned duties and responsibilities. Also, do not forget that we have different types of secretaries and this includes those that require some modicum of technical knowledge e.g., Legal Secretary and Medical Secretary.

Secondly, a secretary is the bedrock of any office – something people choose to overlook until she is unexpectedly out sick and chaos reigns (Greenwood, 2016). A secretary is the repository of institutional knowledge and institutional secrets. He/she is everyone's confidante. If you have ever worked in an office, then you can definitely relate to that statement.

Thirdly, I love writing. It is a hobby and a profession. I have been writing since I was a teenager, when secretaries used to type on typewriters, and in my teenage mind, I developed a profound love and admiration for secretaries since they were the foremost experts in typing. Anyway, despite the fact that the typewriter is now obsolete, you still need to be good in typing on a computer in order to be a good writer.

_____
PETER OVIE AKUS
STUDENT, PATHWAYS COLLEGE

BIBLIOGRAPHY

Bika, N. (n.d.). *Office Clerk job description*. Retrieved from resources.workable.com: https://resources.workable.com/office-clerk-job-description

Bing. (2024, June 22). *Skills of a secretary*. Retrieved from bing.com: https://www.bing.com/search?q=skills+of+a+secretary&form=ANSPH1&refig=e0b98cf01b43474bafd215fec9bff091&pc=U531

Bloom, L. (2018, September 24). *List of the duties of a secretary*. Retrieved from CHRON: https://work.chron.com/list-duties-secretary-6774.html

Career Professionals of Canada. (2020, April 22). *Celebrating All Administrative Professionals*. Retrieved from Careerprocanada.ca: https://careerprocanada.ca/administrative-professionals-day/

CareerOneStop. (2018, July 23). *Secretaries and Administrative Assistants Career Video*. Retrieved from YouTube: https://youtu.be/zDqK9DaCDg4?si=mw7kfH_ESrJdCi-a

Collins Dictionary. (n.d.). *Definition of 'clerk'*. Retrieved from collinsdictionary.com: https://www.collinsdictionary.com/dictionary/english/clerk

Eads, A. (2024, June 3). *21 Important Customer Service Skills (With Resume Example)*. Retrieved from Indeed.com: https://www.indeed.com/career-advice/resumes-cover-letters/customer-service-skills

Emerge. (n.d.). *List of 25 Administrative Job Titles and Roles With Descriptions*. Retrieved from Emerge: https://emerge360.com/blog/list-of-25-administrative-job-titles-and-roles-with-descriptions/

Farmers Insurance. (2017, March 10). *A Day in the life of a Customer Service Representative*. Retrieved from YouTube: https://youtu.be/aeWGQqp-M70?si=xPEP5CGAvHJOXk8a

France, S. (2009). *The Definitive Personal Assistant & Secretarial Handbook*. London: Kogan Page Limited.

Goyette, B. (2022, November 28). *Resume Cat*. Retrieved from resumecat.com: https://resumecat.com/blog/what-does-an-administrative-professional-do

Greenwood, B. (2016, January 17). Why I Always Wanted to Be a Secretary. *The New York Times*, p. 9.

iBuzzle. (n.d.). *Duties and Responsibilities of a Secretary*. Retrieved from ibuzzle.com: https://ibuzzle.com/secretary-duties-responsibilities

Indeed Editorial team. (2022, June 24). *10 Key Secretarial Skills To Use in the Workplace*. Retrieved from Indeed.com: https://www.indeed.com/career-advice/career-development/secretarial-skill

Indeed Editorial Team. (2023, March 10). *What Does a Secretary Do? 12 Essential Secretary Duties*. Retrieved from Indeed.com: https://www.indeed.com/career-advice/finding-a-job/secretary-duties

Indeed Editorial Team. (2023, September 11). *What is an administrator? (with duties and salary)*. Retrieved from ca.indeed.com: https://ca.indeed.com/career-advice/finding-a-job/what-is-an-administrator

Jenna. (n.d.). *Customer Service Representative*. Retrieved from Spotify (Podcast): https://open.spotify.com/show/2zzOn0U4xrDx32ybpgLaDo?si=lR0huLQORNmsBFWtgxhq9g

Kourmentza, E. (n.d.). *Customer Service Representative job description*. Retrieved from resources.workable.com: https://resources.workable.com/customer-service-representative-job-description

LiveAgent. (n.d.). *Customer service duties*. Retrieved from liveagent.com: https://www.liveagent.com/academy/customer-service-duties/

MyJobMag. (n.d.). *Who is a Secretary?* Retrieved from myjobmag.co.za:
   https://www.myjobmag.co.za/job-descriptions/secretary#google_vignette

talent.com. (2024). *Clerk average salary in Canada*. Retrieved from talent.com:
   https://ca.talent.com/salary?job=Clerk

talent.com. (2024). *Customer Service Representative average salary in Canada, 2024*. Retrieved from
   talent.com: https://ca.talent.com/salary?job=customer+service+representative

talent.com. (2024). *Data Entry Assistant average salary salary in Canada, 2024*. Retrieved from
   talent.com: https://ca.talent.com/salary?job=data+entry+assistant

talent.com. (2024). *Receptionist average salary in Canada, 2024*. Retrieved from talent.com:
   https://ca.talent.com/salary?job=receptionist

talent.com. (2024). *Secretary average salary in Canada, 2024*. Retrieved from talent.com:
   https://ca.talent.com/salary?job=Secretary

Taylor, E. (2024, February 27). *Top Secretary Skills That You Should Possess for Career Success*. Retrieved
   from theknowledgeacademy.com: theknowledgeacademy.com:
   https://www.theknowledgeacademy.com/blog/secretary-skills/

Taylor, E. (2024, January 23). *What is a Receptionist? Introduction, Types, & Skills*. Retrieved from
   theknowledgeacademy.com: www.theknowledgeacademy.com/blog/what-is-a-receptionist/

Teal. (n.d.). *What Skills Does a Secretary Need?* Retrieved from tealhq.com:
   https://www.tealhq.com/skills/secretary

Wikipedia contributors. (2024, May 26). *Secretary*. Retrieved from Wikipedia.org:
   https://en.wikipedia.org/wiki/Secretary

ZipRecruiter Marketplace Research Team. (n.d.). *What Is a Data Entry Assistant and How to Become
   One*. Retrieved from Ziprecruiter.com: https://www.ziprecruiter.com/career/Data-Entry-
   Assistant/What-Is-How-to-Become#

©2024.

www.ingramcontent.com/pod-product-compliance
Lightning Source LLC
Chambersburg PA
CBHW070958220526
45471CB00007B/3080